Why Pocket Posters?

Daydream Education, the UK's leading provider of educational posters, has developed a versatile range of colourful and engaging revision guides that break down barriers to learning and encourage independent learning.

Small in size, huge in content!

Designed to engage learners, Pocket Posters are the perfect alternative to the larger text-heavy revision guides. The pocket-sized revision guides simplify key GCSE content into bitesize chunks of information to improve pupils' understanding and boost confidence.

Daydream Education | Unit 1 | Central Park | Western Avenue | Bridgend | CF31 3RH
Tel: 0844 800 1660 | Fax: 0844 800 1664 | www.daydreameducation.co.uk
Chris Malcolm Ltd. t/a Daydream Education. Registered in England and Wales. Company No: 04216204

GCSE Physical Education

Contents

THE SKELETAL SYSTEM

There are more than 200 bones in the human body.

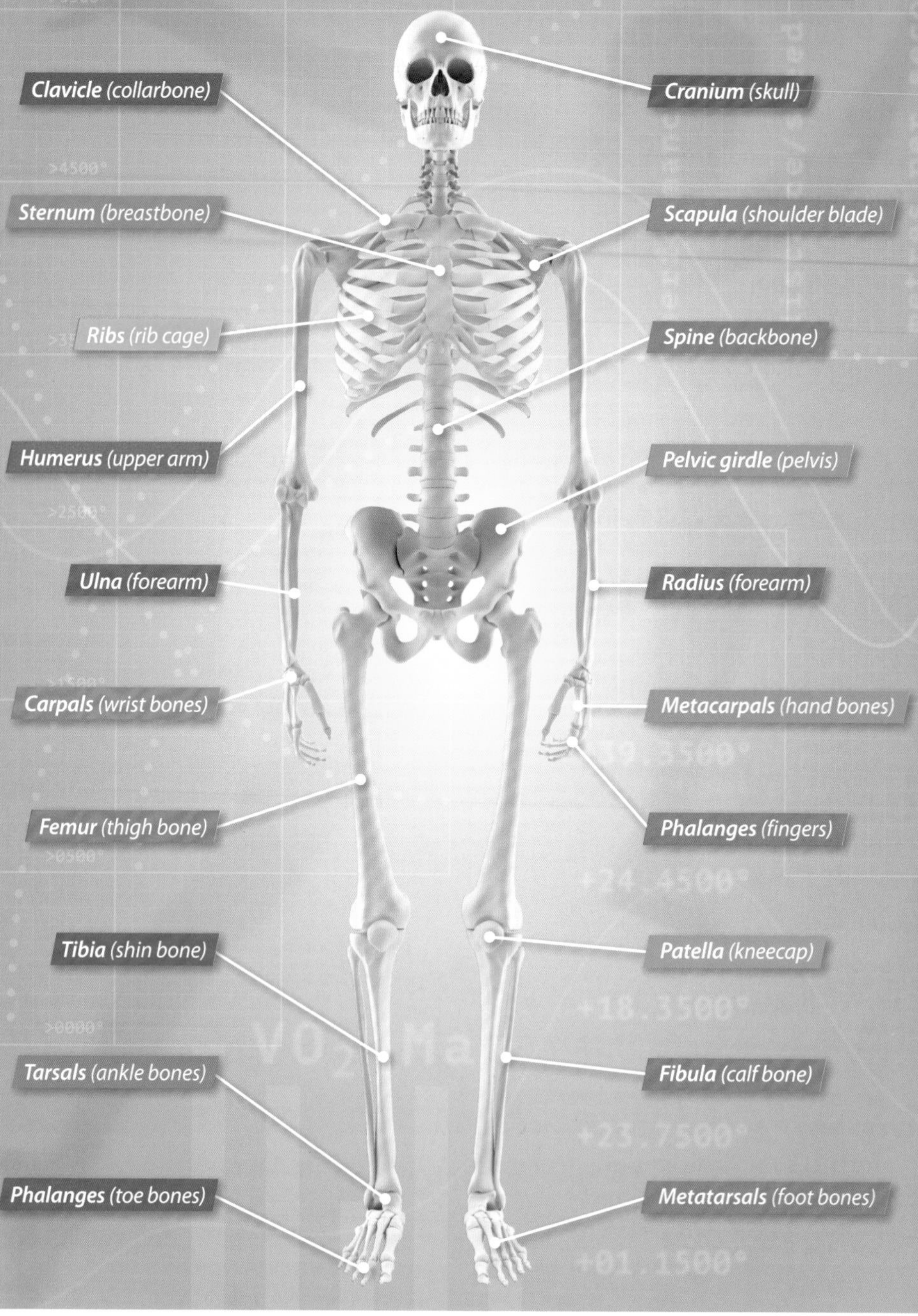

Clavicle (collarbone)

Cranium (skull)

Sternum (breastbone)

Scapula (shoulder blade)

Ribs (rib cage)

Spine (backbone)

Humerus (upper arm)

Pelvic girdle (pelvis)

Ulna (forearm)

Radius (forearm)

Carpals (wrist bones)

Metacarpals (hand bones)

Femur (thigh bone)

Phalanges (fingers)

Tibia (shin bone)

Patella (kneecap)

Tarsals (ankle bones)

Fibula (calf bone)

Phalanges (toe bones)

Metatarsals (foot bones)

THE VERTEBRAL COLUMN

Cervical vertebrae (7)

Thoracic vertebrae (12)

Lumbar vertebrae (5)

Sacrum

Coccyx

FUNCTIONS OF THE SKELETAL SYSTEM

Support
The skeleton supports the body. For example, a backbone enables us to stay upright.

Movement
The skeleton has joints where tendons join muscle to bone. This enables us to move.

Protection
The skeleton helps to protect delicate internal organs from injury.

Blood Production
Blood cells are produced in bone marrow. Red cells transport oxygen, and white cells protect the body.

Mineral Storage
Important minerals, such as calcium and phosphorous, are stored in the bones.

CLASSIFICATION OF BONES

Long Bones
Help translate the force generated by skeletal muscle into mechanical leverage; e.g. femur.

Flat Bones
Help protect the body's internal organs and with muscle attachment; e.g. cranium and sternum.

Short Bones
Help provide support and stability with little movement; e.g. carpals and tarsals.

Irregular Bones
Do not fall into any category but generally help with protection and support; e.g. vertebrae.

JOINTS

A joint is where two or more bones meet. There are three main types of joints:
- **Immovable** *joints (e.g. skull) allow little or no movement.*
- **Partially movable (cartilaginous)** *joints (e.g. spine) allow a limited range of movement.*
- **Freely movable (synovial)** *joints (e.g. elbow, knee) allow free movement.*

FREELY MOVABLE (SYNOVIAL) JOINTS

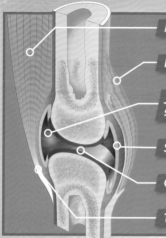

- Muscle
- Ligament
- Joint cavity (contains synovial fluid)
- Synovial membrane
- Cartilage
- Tendon

Bones at freely movable joints are held together by connective tissue.

Ligaments are fibrous tissues that connect bones. They help keep joints stable.

The ends of bones are covered in **cartilage** to aid movement and stop the bones from rubbing together.

Synovial fluid reduces friction at joints, allowing them to move freely.

Tendons connect bones to muscles and enable movement.

TYPES OF SYNOVIAL JOINTS

Hinge

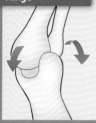

Provides movement in one plane for flexion and extension.

Example: enables flexion and extension at the elbow when performing a pull-up.

Pivot

Provides rotatory movement around a single axis for rotation.

Example: enables rotation of the neck when taking a breath while swimming.

Ball and Socket

Provides 360° rotation and movement in all planes for flexion, extension, abduction, adduction and rotation.

Example: enables rotation at the hip when hurdling.

Condyloid

Provides movement in two planes for flexion, extension, adduction and abduction.

Example: enables extension and flexion at the wrist when dribbling (bouncing) a basketball.

daydream EDUCATION

Flexion

When the angle at a joint **decreases.**

Rotation

A turning or rotating movement around a **single axis.**

Extension

When the angle at a joint **increases.**

Circumduction

The **conical** (circular) movement of a limb extending from the joint.

Abduction

Movement **away** from the midline of the body.

Adduction

Movement **towards** the midline of the body.

Plantar-Flexion

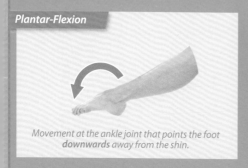

Movement at the ankle joint that points the foot **downwards** away from the shin.

Dorsi-Flexion

Movement at the ankle joint that points the foot **upwards** towards the shin.

HOW MUSCLES WORK

The human body contains more than 600 muscles, of which there are three main types: cardiac, smooth and skeletal muscles.

Cardiac Muscles

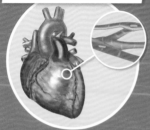

- Involuntarily controlled
- Found in the walls of the heart
- Do not fatigue

Smooth Muscles

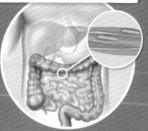

- Involuntarily controlled
- Found in the walls of hollow organs such as the intestines

Skeletal Muscles

- Voluntarily controlled
- Found throughout the body
- Attached to bones by tendons

ANTAGONISTIC MUSCLE PAIRS

Muscles contract to pull bones, but they cannot push them. Therefore, to achieve movement at joints, muscles work in pairs. These muscles are called **antagonistic pairs**.

The biceps and triceps are antagonistic muscles that work together to bend and straighten the arm.

Bending the Arm (flexion)

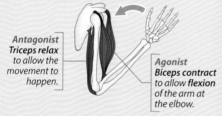

Antagonist Triceps relax to allow the movement to happen.

Agonist Biceps contract to allow **flexion** of the arm at the elbow.

Example: upward phase of a bicep curl

Straightening the Arm (extension)

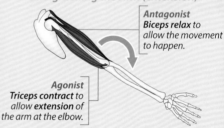

Antagonist Biceps relax to allow the movement to happen.

Agonist Triceps contract to allow **extension** of the arm at the elbow.

Example: downward phase of a bicep curl

The hamstrings and quadriceps are antagonistic muscles that work together to bend and straighten the leg.

Bending the Leg (flexion)

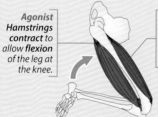

Agonist Hamstrings contract to allow **flexion** of the leg at the knee.

Antagonist Quadriceps relax to allow the movement to happen.

Example: bending the leg before kicking a ball

Straightening the Leg (extension)

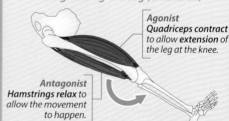

Agonist Quadriceps contract to allow **extension** of the leg at the knee.

Antagonist Hamstrings relax to allow the movement to happen.

Example: straightening the leg to kick a ball

daydream EDUCATION

ISOMETRIC MUSCLE CONTRACTIONS

There is no change in joint angle and muscle length during isometric muscle contractions.

Example: performing a plank.

ISOTONIC MUSCLE CONTRACTIONS

During isotonic muscle contractions, the muscle length changes as it contracts and causes movement. There are two types of contractions.

1 Concentric

Muscles shorten as muscle fibres contract.

Example: the upward (lifting) phase of a biceps curl.

2 Eccentric

Muscles lengthen as muscle fibres contract.

Example: the downward (lowering) phase of a biceps curl.

MUSCLE FIBRES

There are different types of skeletal muscle fibres.

Slow Twitch – Type I

Type I have a slow contraction velocity, are very resistant to fatigue and are capable of repeated low-level contractions by producing large amounts of ATP through oxidative metabolic processes.

Example: marathon runner

Fast Twitch – Type IIA

Type IIA manufacture and split ATP at a fast rate by using both aerobic and anaerobic metabolism and, thus, produce fast, strong muscle contractions. They are more prone to fatigue than type I fibres.

Example: 800m runner

Fast Twitch – Type IIB

Type IIB produce ATP at a slow rate by anaerobic metabolism and break it down very quickly. This results in extremely fast muscle contractions to produce short, fast bursts of power and rapid fatigue.

Example: 100m runner

THE MUSCULAR SYSTEM

Our muscles contract and relax to enable us to move. They also define body shape, protect internal organs, stabilise joints during movement and help maintain posture.

ANTERIOR

POSTERIOR

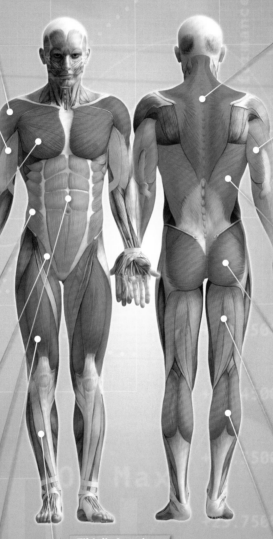

Deltoid
Abduction of the arm at the shoulder. **For example:** Bowling a cricket ball.

Biceps
Flexion of the arm at the elbow joint. **For example:** Pulling the paddle when kayaking.

Pectoralis Major
Responsible for movement around the shoulder joint. **For example:** A chest pass in netball.

External Obliques
Lateral flexion and rotation of the trunk at the waist. **For example:** Preparing to throw a discus.

Hip Flexors
Flexion of the leg at the hip. **For example:** Driving out of the blocks at the start of a sprint.

Abdominals
Flexion of the trunk and assisting with breathing. **For example:** A pike hold in gymnastics.

Quadriceps
Extension of the leg at the knee joint. **For example:** Pushing the pedals when cycling.

Tibialis Anterior
Dorsiflexion of the ankle. **For example:** Lifting of the toes off the ground when walking and running.

Trapezius
Rotation of the scapula and supporting the arm. **For example:** The butterfly stroke in swimming.

Triceps
Extension of the arm at the elbow joint. **For example:** Throwing a javelin.

Latissimus Dorsi
Responsible for movement at the shoulder and lateral flexion of the spine. **For example:** Pulling the oars when rowing.

Gluteal Muscles
Responsible for movement of the leg around the hip. **For example:** Pushing your feet off the ground when sprinting.

Hamstring
Flexion of the leg at the knee joint. **For example:** Lifting your leg to kick a football.

Gastrocnemius
Flexion of the foot at the ankle joint and the leg at the knee joint. **For example:** Taking off when performing a high jump.

12

daydream
EDUCATION

THE RESPIRATORY SYSTEM

The **respiratory system** is the set of organs that is responsible for breathing; the movement of air in and out of the lungs. We breathe to get oxygen into our bodies and carbon dioxide out.

PARTS OF THE RESPIRATORY SYSTEM

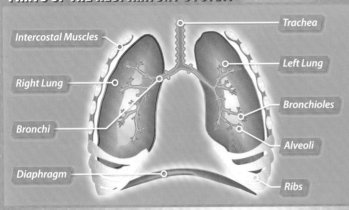

- Intercostal Muscles
- Right Lung
- Bronchi
- Diaphragm
- Trachea
- Left Lung
- Bronchioles
- Alveoli
- Ribs

Total Lung Capacity (TLC)
The volume of air contained in the lungs at the end of a maximal inspiration.

Tidal Volume
The amount of air normally inhaled and exhaled per breath.

Vital Capacity
The maximum volume of air exhaled after the lungs have been filled to capacity.

AEROBIC RESPIRATION

Aerobic respiration occurs in the presence of oxygen, and can be represented by the following equation:

GLUCOSE + OXYGEN = ENERGY + CARBON DIOXIDE + WATER

Inhaling
We inhale to supply our cells with oxygen.

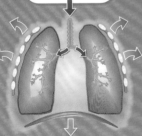

AIR IN
21% Oxygen
0.04% Carbon Dioxide

Chest volume increases as air is sucked into the lungs.

The intercostal muscles contract to expand the rib cage.

The diaphragm contracts and moves down.

Gaseous Exchange
Gaseous exchange takes place in the **alveoli**, where oxygen diffuses from the air to the blood and carbon dioxide diffuses from the blood to the air.

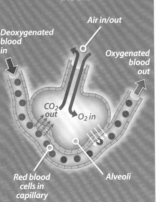

- Deoxygenated blood in
- Air in/out
- Oxygenated blood out
- CO_2 out
- O_2 in
- Red blood cells in capillary
- Alveoli

Exhaling
We exhale to remove carbon dioxide from our bodies.

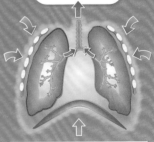

AIR OUT
16% Oxygen
4% Carbon Dioxide

Chest volume decreases as air is forced out of the lungs.

The intercostal muscles relax to reduce chest volume.

The diaphragm relaxes and moves up.

THE CARDIOVASCULAR SYSTEM

THE HEART

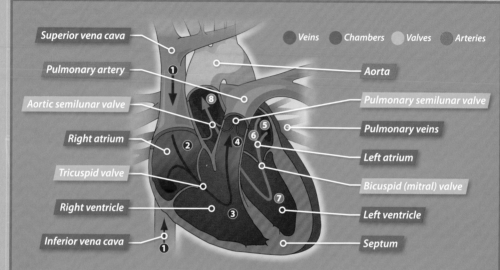

Superior vena cava

Pulmonary artery

Aortic semilunar valve

Right atrium

Tricuspid valve

Right ventricle

Inferior vena cava

● Veins ● Chambers ● Valves ● Arteries

Aorta

Pulmonary semilunar valve

Pulmonary veins

Left atrium

Bicuspid (mitral) valve

Left ventricle

Septum

1 Deoxygenated blood from the body is carried by the vena cava into the right atrium.

2 The right atrium contracts, pushing blood through the tricuspid valve into the right ventricle.

3 The right ventricle contracts, pushing blood through the pulmonary semilunar valve into the pulmonary artery.

4 The blood travels to the lungs, where carbon dioxide is exchanged for oxygen from the air.

5 Oxygenated blood from the lungs is carried by the pulmonary veins into the left atrium.

6 The left atrium contracts, pushing blood through the bicuspid valve into the left ventricle.

7 The left ventricle contracts, pushing blood through the aortic semilunar valve into the aorta.

8 The aorta delivers oxygenated blood to the body, where it is used for energy production.

Heart Rate	Stroke Volume	Cardiac Output
The number of times the heart beats per minute.	The amount of blood pumped out of the left ventricle in one contraction.	The amount of blood pumped out of the left ventricle in one minute.

14

daydream EDUCATION

*The **cardiovascular system** consists of blood vessels and the heart. It is responsible for circulating blood and transporting oxygen, carbon dioxide and nutrients around your body.*

THE BLOOD VESSELS

Arteries

Carry oxygenated blood (except pulmonary artery) at high pressure, from the heart to the body.

Have thick walls made of elastic fibres.

Have narrow channels (lumen) to maintain high pressure.

Veins

Carry deoxygenated blood (except pulmonary veins) at low pressure, from the body to the heart.

Contain valves to prevent backflow and have thin walls.

Have wide channels (lumen) to ease the flow of blood.

Capillaries

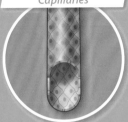

Allow the exchange of materials between tissues and blood.

Have walls that are only one cell thick.

Have channels (lumen) the width of one blood cell, which distort the cells and aid gaseous exchange.

BLOOD

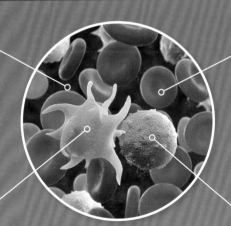

Plasma
The fluid part of blood that carries the other components (platelets, red blood cells and white blood cells) throughout the body.

Red blood cells
Transport oxygen from the lungs to the body's cells, and carbon dioxide from the cells to the lungs; contains haemoglobin, which stores oxygen and carbon dioxide.

Platelets
Tiny cell fragments that clump together to help blood clot and stop bleeding.

White blood cells
Produce antibodies to fight against infectious diseases.

The Function of Blood During Exercise

Transports nutrients and water throughout the body	Delivers **oxygen** to the working muscles	Removes **waste**, including carbon dioxide	Removes heat (**temperature regulation**)	**Dilutes** or carries away lactic acid

daydream EDUCATION

AEROBIC RESPIRATION

Aerobic respiration *is a form of respiration that uses oxygen.*

HOW IT WORKS

In aerobic respiration, oxygen and glucose are used to create energy.

GLUCOSE + OXYGEN ⟶ CARBON DIOXIDE + WATER + ENERGY

Glucose is broken down to produce energy, carbon dioxide and water.

If there is insufficient oxygen for aerobic respiration, anaerobic respiration takes place.

SPORTING RELEVANCE

As long as your body has enough oxygen to meet the demands of your cells, your body will produce energy aerobically. Therefore, aerobic respiration is used in low- to medium-intensity activities, such as long-distance running, swimming, cycling and rowing.

Aerobic respiration is also essential for most individual and team sports, including dancing, boxing, basketball, hockey and squash.

ENERGY SOURCES

In order to provide energy, your body also needs a source of fuel.

Carbohydrates

Carbohydrates are the body's main fuel source. They are used during moderate-intensity aerobic activities and high-intensity anaerobic activities.

Fats

Fats contain more energy than carbohydrates but are digested slower. They are used as fuel for low-intensity aerobic activities.

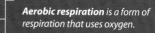 **daydream** EDUCATION

ANAEROBIC RESPIRATION

Anaerobic respiration is a type of respiration that does not use oxygen. It is used when there is not enough oxygen for aerobic respiration.

HOW IT WORKS

Anaerobic Respiration takes place when the body is unable to supply muscles with sufficient oxygen for aerobic respiration. It is represented by the following equation:

$$GLUCOSE \longrightarrow ENERGY + LACTIC\ ACID$$

Glucose is broken down to produce **energy** and **lactic acid**.

Anaerobic respiration produces approximately 5–10% of the energy that can be produced through aerobic respiration. Lactic acid can cause muscle pain and cramps.

OXYGEN DEBT AND RECOVERY

Oxygen debt refers to the extra oxygen that is needed after intense anaerobic exercise to convert lactic acid into waste products (carbon dioxide and water), that can be removed from the body.

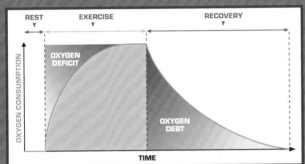

To facilitate this process we:

- Take deeper or quicker breaths to help with the intake of oxygen and removal of carbon dioxide.

- Perspire to lower the body's temperature and remove excess water through sweat.

- Excrete excess water and other waste products through urine and faeces.

A good cool-down will help with the breakdown and dispersal of lactic acid.

SPORTING RELEVANCE

Anaerobic respiration is used during intense exercises that require a short, sharp burst of effort.

Hockey	100m Sprint	Weightlifting	Javelin

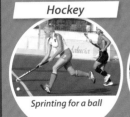

Sprinting for a ball | *Running 100 metres as fast as possible* | *Lifting a weight in one explosive movement* | *Throwing the javelin as far as possible*

THE LONG-TERM EFFECTS OF EXERCISE

THE RESPIRATORY SYSTEM

The following adaptations result from long-term exercise and make the respiratory system stronger, enabling it to take in and deliver more oxygen to the working muscles.

- Lung volume increases as the diaphragm and intercostal muscles become stronger.

- Tidal volume, the volume of air inhaled and exhaled in each breath, increases.

- A greater number of capillaries grow around the alveoli, making gaseous exchange more efficient.

- VO_2 max, the maximum volume of oxygen the body can use per minute, increases.

- Vital capacity, the maximum volume of air exhaled after the lungs have been filled to capacity, increases.

THE MUSCULOSKELETAL SYSTEM

The following adaptations result from long-term exercise and make the musculoskeletal system stronger, enabling it to work harder for longer and reducing the risk of injury.

- Muscular endurance and strength improves.

- Muscle size increases (hypertrophy).

- Bones become denser and stronger as more calcium is produced.

- Stretching makes tendons stronger and ligaments more flexible, improving joint stability.

- Weight-bearing exercises help reduce the risk of osteoporosis.

18

daydream EDUCATION

Once you have trained regularly (more than once a week) for a prolonged period of time (approx. 6 weeks +) your body will adapt and get stronger, enabling you to train for longer and at a higher intensity.

THE CARDIOVASCULAR SYSTEM

The following adaptations result from long-term exercise and make the cardiovascular system stronger, enabling it to circulate blood around the body more efficiently.

- The heart becomes bigger and stronger, and can therefore pump more blood around the body.
- Resting stroke volume, the amount of blood pumped out of the left ventricle in one contraction, increases.
- Maximum cardiac output, the amount of blood pumped out of the left ventricle in one minute, increases.
- The number of red blood cells (haemoglobin) increases to cope with the demands of carrying extra oxygen.
- Resting heart rate decreases, and less recovery time is needed after exercise.
- Capillary density (capillarisation) increases.
- Arteries and veins become more elastic, reducing blood pressure.

HEALTH & FITNESS BENEFITS

The adaptations that occur as a result of long-term exercise will help you do the following:

- Train harder for longer

- Improve overall health and performance

- Reduce the risk of injury

- Improve recovery time

- Improve flexibility

Remember to rest between training sessions to give your body time to recover and enable adaptations to occur.

daydream EDUCATION

Photocopying or scanning this image is a breach of copyright law.

THE SHORT-TERM EFFECTS OF EXERCISE

When we exercise, the working muscles require more oxygen and the following changes occur:

RESPIRATORY SYSTEM

The respiratory system responds to physical activity by increasing the rate and depth of breathing to increase oxygen delivery and carbon dioxide removal.

- Respiratory rate, the number of breaths per minute, increases.

- Tidal volume, the volume of air inhaled and exhaled in one breath, increases.

- The rate of gaseous exchange increases.

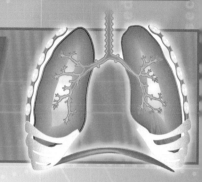

CARDIOVASCULAR SYSTEM

During physical activity, blood is redistributed to increase the blood flow to the working muscles. This process is called vascular shunting.

- Heart rate, the number of heart beats per minute, increases.

- Stroke volume, the amount of blood pumped out of the left ventricle in one contraction, increases.

- Cardiac output, the volume of blood pumped by the heart per minute, increases.

- **Vasodilation** - blood vessels leading to the working muscles open (dilate) to increase blood flow.

- **Vasoconstriction** - blood vessels leading to the digestive system close (constrict) to reduce blood flow.

- Blood vessels near the skin open to allow heat to escape.

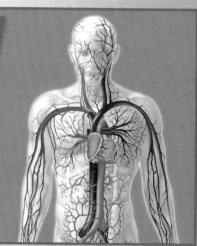

MUSCULAR SYSTEM

During exercise, working muscles require an increased supply of oxygen and glucose to create energy in the form of adenosine triphosphate (ATP).

- Muscle contractions increase.

- Carbon dioxide production increases.

- Where oxygen is not available, lactic acid is created.

- Muscles fatigue.

- Muscle temperature increases.

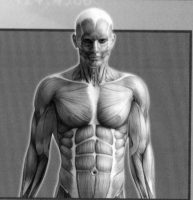

20

LEVER SYSTEMS

*Muscles and bones work together to form **levers**. A lever is a rigid rod (usually a bone) that turns about a **pivot** (usually a joint). Levers can turn a small force into a bigger force. This is known as **mechanical advantage**.*

If the fulcrum is closer to the effort than to the load, there will be a **mechanical disadvantage** and the output force will be less than the input force.

All levers are made up of three parts:

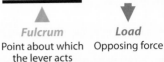

Effort
Input force

Fulcrum
Point about which the lever acts

Load
Opposing force

If the fulcrum is closer to the load than to the effort, there will be a **mechanical advantage** and the output force will be greater than the input force.

FIRST-CLASS LEVERS

The fulcrum is positioned between the effort and the load.

When you lift your head to look up:

- The joint where your skull meets your spinal column acts as the fulcrum.

- The weight of your head is the load.

- The muscles at the top of your neck provide the effort to lift your head.

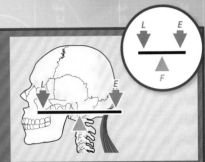

SECOND-CLASS LEVERS

The load is positioned between the fulcrum and the effort.

When you push off when jumping:

- The joints in your toes act as the fulcrum.

- The weight of your body is the load.

- Your calf muscles provide the effort to lift your body.

In this lever, the load is always closer to the fulcrum than the effort so there is always a **mechanical advantage**.

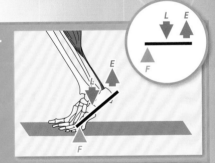

THIRD-CLASS LEVERS

The effort is positioned between the fulcrum and the load.

When you perform a biceps curl:

- Your elbow joint acts as the fulcrum.

- The weight of the dumbbell is the load.

- Your biceps provide the effort to lift the dumbbell.

In this lever, the effort is always closer to the fulcrum than the load so there is always a **mechanical disadvantage**.

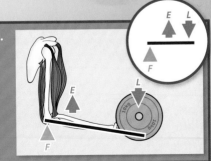

21

PLANES & AXES OF MOVEMENT

PLANES

Sagittal Plane
Runs vertically from front to back and divides the body into right and left parts.

Flexion and extension are movements in this plane. They are forward or backward movements parallel to the plane. Examples include a biceps curl, kicking a ball and running.

Movement **in the sagittal plane** takes place **about the frontal axis**.

Frontal Plane
Runs vertically from side to side and divides the body into anterior (front) and posterior (back) parts.

Abduction and adduction are movements in this plane. They are side movements parallel to the plane. Examples include a star jump, lateral raise and side lunge.

Movement **in the frontal plane** takes place **about the sagittal axis**.

Transverse Plane
Runs horizontally and divides the body into superior (top) and inferior (bottom) parts.

Rotation takes place in this plane. Examples include a golf swing, discus throw or wood-chop.

Movement **in the transverse plane** takes place **about the vertical axis**.

daydream
EDUCATION

Movement takes place **in a plane** and **about an axis**.

Planes - There are three imaginary planes that pass through the body to represent dynamic planes of movement.

Axes - An axis is a straight line around which an object rotates. There are three axes of rotation.

AXES

EXAMPLES

Frontal Axis
Runs horizontally from side to side and is perpendicular to the sagittal plane.

A front or back somersault takes place in the sagittal plane about the frontal axis.

Sagittal Axis
Runs horizontally from front to back and is perpendicular to the frontal plane.

A cartwheel takes place in the frontal plane about the sagittal axis.

Vertical Axis
Runs vertically and is perpendicular to the transverse plane.

A pirouette takes place in the transverse plane about the vertical axis.

daydream EDUCATION

CARDIOVASCULAR FITNESS

*Cardiovascular Fitness is the ability to exercise the whole body for **prolonged periods of time, without tiring**. It is a Health-Related component of physical fitness.*

The **cardiovascular system**, which consists of the heart (cardio) and blood vessels (vascular), circulates blood around the body to deliver oxygen for energy production.

COOPER'S 12-MINUTE RUN

This test entails running as far as possible in 12 minutes, preferably around a 200- or 400-metre track so it easy to record the distance covered.

After you have finished, calculate your distance in metres and compare your result to the normative data for the Cooper's 12-minute run test as shown in the table below.

Age	Excellent	Good	Average	Fair	Poor
Male					
15 – 16	>2,800	>2,500	>2,300	>2,200	<2,200
17 – 19	>3,000	>2,700	>2,500	>2,300	<2,300
Female					
15 – 16	>2,100	>2,000	>1,700	>1,600	<1,600
17 – 19	>2,300	>2,100	>1,800	>1,700	<1,700

An Olympic standard 5,000 m runner would expect to run over 4,000 metres in the 12 minutes.

IMPROVING YOUR CARDIOVASCULAR FITNESS

You can improve your cardiovascular fitness by working in your aerobic training zone. This is found between 60% and 80% of your **maximum heart rate** (MHR = 220 – age).

You should exercise in this zone for at least 20 minutes. However, timing will vary depending on your fitness level and training goals.

Continuous, fartlek and circuit training are good methods for helping improve cardiovascular fitness.

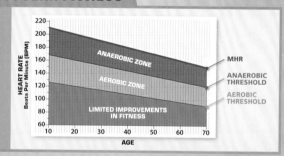

SPORTING RELEVANCE

Cardiovascular endurance is essential for sports that involve **prolonged periods of exercise**, such as long-distance running, swimming, cycling and rowing. It is also essential for most individual and team sports, including dancing, boxing, basketball, rugby and squash.

daydream
EDUCATION

STRENGTH

Strength involves applying a **force** to overcome a resistance. It is a **Health-Related** component of physical fitness.

There are three main types of **Muscular Strength:**

Static	Dynamic	Explosive
To apply a force to a fixed object. Muscle length stays the same (isometric contraction).	To repeatedly apply a force over a sustained period. Muscle length alters frequently over a period of time.	To apply a force in one fast movement. Muscles contract at a high speed.

HAND GRIP DYNAMOMETER TEST

This test involves squeezing the dynamometer grips together with maximum effort, and measures forearm and hand strength. Normative data for the hand grip test is shown in the table below.

Gender	Age	Excellent	Good	Average	Fair	Poor
Male	16-19	>56	56-51	50.9-45	44.9-39	<39
Female	16-19	>36	36-31	30.9-25	24.9-19	<19

IMPROVING MUSCULAR STRENGTH

Weight training is great way to improve muscular strength. Below is a simple three-day training programme for improving overall strength. Aim to perform 3-4 sets of 4-6 repetitions at 80% of your 1-rep max for each exercise. Always perform a full warm-up and use the correct technique.

Day	Body Parts	Exercise 1	Exercise 2	Exercise 3	Exercise 4
1	Chest, triceps, shoulders	Bench press /Press-ups	Dumbbell flys	Shoulder press	Triceps extensions/Dips
2	Back, biceps, abdominals	Lat pulldowns/ Pull-ups	Biceps curls	Seated rows	Crunches/Leg raises/V-sits
3	Legs	Squats	Lunges	Leg press	Calf raises

SPORTING RELEVANCE

Static	Dynamic	Explosive

A rugby scrum
Handstand
Tug of war

Cycling
Swimming
Rock climbing

Shot-put
Throwing a ball
Weight lifting

daydream EDUCATION

MUSCULAR ENDURANCE

Muscular Endurance is the ability of a voluntary muscle group or muscle to **work for a prolonged period of time without tiring.** It is a Health-Related component of physical fitness.

ABDOMINAL CURL TEST

This test entails performing sit-ups in time to beeps, which are set to a speed of 20 beeps per minute.

You must perform as many sit-ups as possible until you are unable to keep in time with the beeps.

The number of sit-ups completed is your score.

Normative data for the abdominal curl test is shown in the table below.

Gender	Age	Excellent	Good	Average	Fair	Poor
Male	16 – 19	>55	55 – 40	39.9 – 30	29.9 – 20	<20
Female	16 – 19	>45	45 – 35	34.9 – 25	24.9 – 15	<15

IMPROVING YOUR MUSCULAR ENDURANCE

You can improve your muscular endurance by training your muscles to exercise for longer periods of time.

Circuit, fartlek and weight training are all great types of training that can help improve muscular endurance.

SPORTING RELEVANCE

Muscular endurance is needed in a huge variety of sporting activities. In addition to long-distance events such as running, swimming, rowing and cycling, muscular endurance is a key attribute in many team and individual sports such as football, netball, tennis and skiing.

Swimming

Cycling

Boxing

Rowing

daydream EDUCATION

FLEXIBILITY

Flexibility is the range of movement around a joint. It is a **Health-Related** component of physical fitness.

SIT AND REACH TEST

The **Sit and Reach Test** measures lower back and hamstring flexibility.

To perform this test, sit with your legs straight in front of you and the soles of your feet against the box. Reach forward as far as you can, hold for three seconds and record the distance reached in centimetres.

Normative data for the sit and reach test is shown in the table below.

Gender	Age	Excellent	Good	Average	Fair	Poor
Male	16-19	>14	14-11	10.9-7	6.9-4	<4
Female	16-19	>15	15-12	11.9-7	6.9-4	<4

IMPROVING FLEXIBILITY

You can improve your flexibility through **static and dynamic stretching**. Stretching improves range of movement, reduces the chance of injury and helps enhance performance. Therefore, it should play an important part in any training programme, warm-up and cool-down.

SPORTING RELEVANCE

Flexibility is needed in most sporting activities, in particular gymnastics and dance. Below are some examples of sporting activities in which **good flexibility** is vital.

Tennis Serve

Hurdles

Gymnastic Splits

Swimming

Shoulders & arms

Hips & legs

Hips & legs

Shoulders & arms

daydream EDUCATION

27

BODY COMPOSITION

*Body Composition is the **percentage of body weight that is fat, muscle and bone**. It is a **Health-Related** component of physical fitness.*

SOMATOTYPING

Identifying body type is called **somatotyping**.

There are three extreme somatotypes:

Most people lie somewhere in between the extreme body types.

Extreme Endomorph	*Extreme Mesomorph*	*Extreme Ectomorph*
Wide hips Pear-shaped body Stores fat easily	Wide shoulders Narrow hips Builds muscle easily	Narrow shoulders Narrow hips Struggles to store fat and build muscle

SKINFOLD CALIPER

Body composition can be measured using a skinfold caliper. Take a pinch of skin with your index finger and thumb, and read the measurements with the caliper.

Take measurements from your:
Waist (suprailiac) • **Front arm** (biceps) • **Back arm** (triceps) • **Back** (subscapula)

The average 18–20 year old male has 14–19% body fat, and the average 18–20 year old female has 23–28%. Elite athletes have lower than average body fat percentages, with males having 6–12% and females having 15–21%.

SPORTING RELEVANCE

Different body types are suited to different sports.

Endomorph	*Mesomorph*	*Ectomorph*

Suited to activities that involve power, or where weight is advantageous (e.g. power-lifting and shot-put).	*Suited to activities that require strength, agility or speed (e.g. sprinting, hockey and boxing).*	*Suited to endurance activities (e.g. long-distance running and cycling).*

daydream EDUCATION

AGILITY

*Agility is the ability to **change direction quickly and accurately**, combining **speed, balance, power** and **coordination**. It is a **Skill-Related** component of physical fitness.*

THE ILLINOIS AGILITY TEST

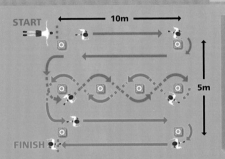

START — 10m — 5m — FINISH

In the **Illinois Agility Test**, the participant runs a set route around a course as quickly as possible.

To complete the test, lie face down at the start cone and on the command 'go', jump up and complete the course (shown in the picture) as quickly as possible. Your score is based on the time (in seconds) it takes you to complete the course.

Normative data for the Illinois agility test is shown in the table below.

Gender	Age	Excellent	Good	Average	Fair	Poor
Male	16-19	<15.2	15.2-16.1	16.2-18.1	18.2-19.3	>19.3
Female	16-19	<17	17-17.9	18-21.7	21.8-23	>23

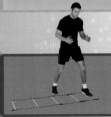

IMPROVING AGILITY

There are various training methods that can help improve agility. SAQ training and hurdle/ladder drills are great for improving speed, balance, power and coordination. Training can also be tailored to specific sports, for example, dribbling a football around a circuit as fast as possible.

SPORTING RELEVANCE

The ability to change direction quickly is required in most sports. Below are some examples of sporting activities in which good agility is essential.

Basketball
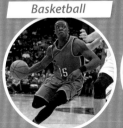

Rugby

Netball

Badminton

BALANCE

*Balance is the ability to **retain centre of mass** (gravity) above the base of support whilst stationary (static) or moving (dynamic). It is a **Skill-Related** component of physical fitness.*

STORK TEST

The **Stork Test** measures **static balance**.

Stand with your hands on your hips, and place the sole of your right foot against the inside of your left knee, or vice versa. Rise up on the toes of your standing leg, and hold your balance for as long as possible. Record your time in seconds.

Normative data for the stork test is shown in the table below.

Gender	Age	Excellent	Good	Average	Fair	Poor
Male	16 – 19	>50	49.9 – 40	39.9 – 30	29.9 – 20	<20
Female	16 – 19	>30	29.9 – 23	22.9 – 16	15.9 – 10	<10

IMPROVING BALANCE

There are various training methods that can help improve static and dynamic balance, including SAQ training and hurdle/ladder drills.

Training your core muscles will also help you improve muscular balance. Try performing exercises on an exercise ball or bosu ball.

SPORTING RELEVANCE

Balance is a key attribute in most sports, from simple actions such as running to more complex activities such as gymnastics.

Gymnastics *Skiing* *Dance* *Discus*

30

daydream EDUCATION

COORDINATION

*Coordination is the ability to use a **combination of body parts and senses** at the same time to produce smooth and efficient movements. It is a **Skill-Related** component of physical fitness.*

ALTERNATE HAND WALL THROW

The **Alternate Hand Wall Throw** measures hand-eye coordination.

To perform the test, stand two metres from a wall, throw a ball against the wall with one hand and catch it with your other hand. Repeat this with alternate hands and record the number of successful catches in 30 seconds.

Normative data for the alternate hand wall throw test is shown in the table below.

Excellent	Good	Average	Fair	Poor
>35	34 – 31	30 – 25	24 – 20	<20

IMPROVING COORDINATION

Coordination and motor skills form the basis of all sports. Fine motor skills involve small, precise movements, such as a snooker shot, whereas gross motor skills involve large muscle movements, such as a triple jump. Both types of motor skills can be improved through practice and training.

Ladder drills are a great way of improving coordination and agility.

SPORTING RELEVANCE

Most sports require a degree of coordination. Good coordination will help improve performance.

Hockey	*Squash*	*Netball*	*Football*

Controlling the ball	Hitting the ball	Catching the ball	Dribbling the ball

POWER

Power is the **combination of strength and speed of movement**. To generate power you need good balance and coordination. Power is a *Skill-Related* component of physical fitness.

VERTICAL JUMP TEST

① ② ③

The **Vertical Jump Test** measures leg power.

To perform the test, stand side on to a wall, reach up as far as you can with your hand closest to the wall and mark your standing reach height. Then, driving with your arms and legs, jump as high as you can and touch the wall at the highest point.

The difference between your standing and jumping reach heights in centimetres is your score.

Normative data for the vertical jump test is shown in the table below.

Gender	Age	Excellent	Good	Average	Fair	Poor
Male	16 – 19	>65	65 – 50	49.9 – 40	39.9 – 30	<30
	>19	>70	70 – 56	55.9 – 41	40.9 – 30	<30
Female	16 – 19	>58	58 – 47	46.9 – 36	35.9 – 26	<26
	>19	>60	60 – 46	45.9 – 31	30.9 – 20	<20

IMPROVING POWER

You can improve power through training that involves explosive and dynamic movements, such as plyometrics or weight training using heavy weights and low repetitions.

SPORTING RELEVANCE

Most sports require a degree of power, and increasing your power can help improve performance.

Football	Baseball	Javelin	Weightlifting

Kicking the ball

Hitting the ball

Throwing the javelin

Pressing the weight

daydream EDUCATION

REACTION TIME

Reaction Time is the **time taken** to react to a **stimulus**. It is a **Skill-Related** component of physical fitness.

RULER DROP TEST

The **Ruler Drop Test** measures reaction time. The test is performed with a partner who holds the ruler.

As your partner holds the ruler, stand with your hand in front of you and position the ruler in-between your index finger and thumb. The top of your index finger should be level with 0 cms on the ruler.

Your partner then drops the ruler, and you must catch the ruler as quickly as possible. Measure the point at which you caught the ruler from the top of your thumb. Repeat two more times, and then take an average of your three scores.

Normative data for the ruler drop test is shown in the table below.

Excellent	Good	Average	Fair	Poor
<7.5	<16	<20	<28	>28

IMPROVING REACTION TIME

Reaction time is an intrinsic skill. However, it can be improved through practice. For example, a sprinter can practise reacting to a starting pistol, or a football goalkeeper can practise reacting to a shot. Reaction time can also be improved by reading the situation and anticipating the stimuli.

SPORTING RELEVANCE

The ability to react quickly to a stimulus is required in most sports.

Cricket	Table Tennis	Football	Rugby

A batsman reacting to a quick bowl

A player reacting to a serve

A goalkeeper reacting to a shot

A player reacting to a sidestep

SPEED

*Speed is the ability to **move your body, or part of your body, quickly**. It is a **Skill-Related** component of physical fitness.*

30-METRE DASH

The **30 Metre Dash** is used to measure maximum sprint speed.

It involves running 30 metres as fast as possible, with a rolling start (already running). Time is recorded in seconds.

Normative data for the 30–metre dash test (in seconds) is shown in the table below.

Gender	Age	Excellent	Good	Average	Fair	Poor
Male	16 – 19	<4	4 – 4.2	4.21 – 4.4	4.41 – 4.6	>4.6
Female	16 – 19	<4	4 – 4.6	4.61 – 4.8	4.81 – 5	>5.0

Once your time has been recorded, you can calculate your speed in metres per second.

$$\text{Your time: 4.4} \quad \frac{\text{Distance}}{\text{Time}} = \frac{30 \text{ m}}{4.4 \text{ s}} \quad \text{Your speed: 6.82 m/s}$$

IMPROVING SPEED

Speed can be improved through training methods that concentrate on strength, power and technique.

Video analysis and practising the activity will improve technique, whereas interval, weight and plyometric training will improve strength and power.

Flexibility training can also help improve speed by increasing the range of movement of joints.

SPORTING RELEVANCE

Speed is essential in sport, especially for racing. However, it is also needed for specific movements. For example, cricket bowlers need to move their arms fast to bowl the ball as quickly as possible.

Boxing	Rugby	Javelin	Hockey

Throwing a punch

Racing for a ball

Throwing the javelin

Chasing after a ball

daydream EDUCATION

PRINCIPLES OF TRAINING

*Training should be matched to the individual needs of the performer. When designing a training programme, the **Principles of Training** should be applied.*

SPECIFICITY

Training programmes must be specific to the chosen activity.

Tailoring training programmes to the needs of performers will ensure that they train the correct muscles and body systems for their chosen activity. For example, the training needs of a marathon runner will differ from those of a weightlifter.

PROGRESSIVE OVERLOAD

To improve and to continue to develop, a training programme must gradually be made more difficult.

As a performer becomes fitter, his or her training programme needs to be made more difficult to ensure fitness gains continue.

The increase in intensity must be gradual because increasing the intensity too quickly can increase the risk of injury.

FITT

To become fitter, you must progressively work your body harder than normal. This can be achieved by applying the **FITT** principles.

Frequency – how often you exercise

Intensity – how hard you exercise

Time – how long you exercise

Type – how your training matches your chosen activity

OVERTRAINING

You must give your body's systems adequate time to recover (repair and adapt) following a training session or you run the risk of overtraining.

Rest is the time allowed for recovery. Recovery is the time required to repair damage caused during exercise. Important elements of rest and recovery include sleep, good nutrition and hydration.

REVERSIBILITY

Exercise improves fitness. Fitness levels drop if regular exercise is stopped.

If you train, your muscles get bigger (hypertrophy). Alternatively, if you stop training, your muscles get smaller (atrophy).

Although rest periods are an essential element of recovery, extended rest periods result in a reduction of physical fitness at a rate much higher than it was achieved. If you don't use it, you lose it!

> **Remember!**
>
> *To avoid injury, all training programmes should include a full **warm-up** and **cool-down**.*

WARM UP & COOL DOWN

All exercise sessions, whether aerobic or anaerobic, should consist of a warm-up, a main exercise session and a cool-down.

WARM-UP

A warm-up safely prepares the body, physically and mentally, for more strenuous activity and reduces the likelihood of injury. Cool muscles do not absorb nutrients, oxygen or impact as well as warm muscles.

A warm-up should be specific to your chosen activity, and include the following:

A Pulse Raiser

Stretching

Drills

Raising your pulse through gentle aerobic activity will help increase your heart rate and body temperature.

Static and dynamic stretching helps improve range of movement, mobilise joints and maintain body temperature.

A warm-up should include activity-specific drills such as low-intensity golf swings or tennis serves.

A good warm-up should last 10-20 minutes and involve a gradual increase in intensity.

MAIN SESSION

The main session can be a training programme or a game or match. If the main session is a training programme, it is vital to ensure it is tailored to meet your specific needs and incorporates the principles of training.

COOL-DOWN

An effective cool-down assists recovery, reduces heart rate and helps with the removal of lactic acid and other waste products.

Like a warm-up, a cool-down should include light cardio exercise and stretching. This helps to slowly return the heart rate and breathing rate to resting rates, decrease muscle tension and return muscles to a pre-exercise state.

36

daydream EDUCATION

TRAINING ZONES & THRESHOLDS

By understanding training zones and thresholds, sports performers can ensure that they train at the correct intensity to work the desired energy system. This helps them create specific training programmes that match their goals.

MONITORING HEART RATE

Training zones and thresholds are determined by percentages of **maximum heart rate (MHR)** which can be calculated using the following formula:

MAXIMUM HEART RATE = 220 – YOUR AGE

The most accurate way to measure your heart rate is with a heart rate monitor. Alternatively, you can measure it manually by finding your pulse in your wrist or neck and counting the number of times your heart beats in one minute.

TRAINING THRESHOLDS

Training zones and thresholds are determined by percentage of MHR.

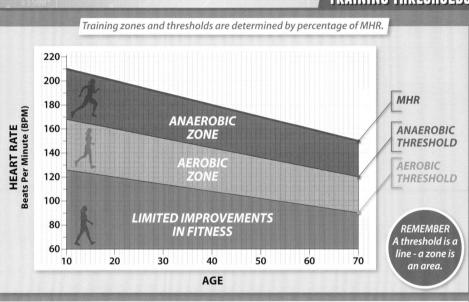

MHR

ANAEROBIC THRESHOLD

AEROBIC THRESHOLD

REMEMBER
A threshold is a line - a zone is an area.

Zone	Intensity	% of MHR	Why train in this zone	Examples
Anaerobic	High to Very High	80%+	Anaerobic activity promotes strength, speed and power, and improves the body's ability to dispose of lactic acid. Training time is short because of the high intensity.	Activities that require all-out effort such as weightlifting and sprinting.
Aerobic	Light to Moderate	60-80%	Aerobic activity improves cardiovascular fitness and aerobic capacity. The aerobic energy system can work for long periods.	Long-distance swimming, jogging and rowing.
Limited Improvement	Very Light	Below 60%	Training below the aerobic threshold results in limited fitness improvements. You would train in this zone when first starting an exercise programme or warming up.	Gentle walk.

TRAINING METHODS

Different training methods are suited to different sports and activities. As a result, sports performers must select training methods that suit, or can be adapted, to their chosen activity.

CONTINUOUS

Involves long periods of moderate exercise without rest. Work for at least 20 minutes at 60–80% of maximum heart rate.

Suitable for endurance events such as long-distance running or cycling.

+ Improves aerobic fitness, cardiovascular fitness and muscular endurance
+ Easy to monitor work rate and progression
+ Limited equipment or facilities required

− Does not develop other components of fitness
− Time-consuming
− Can become repetitive and boring

FARTLEK (SPEED PLAY)

A continuous workout involving changes in speed and/or terrain.

Suitable for sports involving constant changes in intensity, such as netball, rugby, hockey and basketball.

+ Develops both aerobic and anaerobic systems
+ Improves cardiovascular fitness and muscular endurance
+ Can be adapted to suit most sports and improve other components of fitness

− Can become repetitive and boring
− Difficult to monitor work rate and progression
− Can be difficult to maintain work rate

INTERVAL

Involves alternating periods of work and rest.

Suitable for sports involving alternating periods of intense effort and rest, such as basketball, rugby, hockey and netball.

+ Develops both aerobic and anaerobic systems
+ Can be adapted to suit specific sports and improve other components of fitness
+ Easy to monitor work rate and progression

− Can become repetitive and boring
− Can be difficult to maintain work rate

daydream EDUCATION

CIRCUIT

A series of exercises performed in a circuit that can be adapted to suit most sports.

Excellent for general fitness; can also incorporate skills, such as passing or dribbling a ball in basketball or football.

+ Develops both aerobic and anaerobic systems
+ Can be adapted to suit specific sports and improve other components of fitness
+ Easy to monitor work rate and progression

− Can require lots of equipment and time to set up
− Requires a lot of space
− Can be difficult to maintain work rate

WEIGHT TRAINING

A type of interval training that involves using weights as a form of of resistance; can be used to aid recovery after injury.

Suitable for all activities, especially those involving power and strength, such as shot-put, sprinting, rugby and wrestling.

+ Improves muscular strength, endurance, size and power
+ High reps, low weight for muscular endurance
+ Low reps, high weight for strength and power
+ Easy to monitor work rate and progression

− Requires specialist equipment
− Can cause serious injury if incorrect techniques are used

PLYOMETRICS

Exercises in which muscles exert maximum force in short intervals of time, with the goal of increasing power; also known as jump training.

Suitable for activities that require explosive strength and power, such as sprinting, track and field events, football and rugby.

+ Improves muscular strength, power and speed
+ Can utilize the whole body
+ No equipment required

− Very demanding on muscles and joints
− High risk of injury

In addition to these training methods, various activities and classes, such as BodyPump, aerobics, Pilates, yoga and spinning can help improve fitness.

SAFETY IN SPORT

All physical activity involves the risk of injury. Therefore, it is important to identify these risks and how they can be reduced.

Before starting an exercise programme, complete a Physical Activity Readiness Questionnaire (PAR-Q) to ensure that it is suitable. If you answer yes to any of the questions, you should discontinue the programme and arrange to see your doctor.

B BODY

Always complete a full warm-up and cool-down.
Warm-up: Perform a light aerobic activity to increase blood flow, and stretch muscles to avoid injury.
Cool-down: Gradually reduce the level of activity to help with the dispersal of lactic acid and avoid muscle stiffness.

R RULES

Many sports have rules that have been implemented to improve safety and to protect the participants.
Referees and umpires oversee sporting activities to ensure that participants adhere to the rules, which reduces the risk of injury.

E EQUIPMENT

Always check equipment and facilities before a sporting activity to ensure they are safe and in good working order.
Also, many sports use safety equipment to prevent injury – for example, post protectors in rugby.

A ABILITY

Ability levels vary greatly in sport. Therefore, it is important to group performers of similar ability to ensure there is balanced competition.
Age, weight and skill level should be used to identify ability levels and group participants, particularly in contact activities.

K KIT

To avoid injury in sport, it is imperative that the appropriate clothing and footwear are worn.
For example, football players must wear shin pads and studded boots, whereas cricketers have to wear helmets, gloves and various other padding whilst batting.

S SURFACE

Before a sporting activity, evaluate the environment and perform a risk assessment to ensure it is safe for the activity.
Ensure the surface is free from litter, broken glass, potholes and other potential hazards. It is also important to check that the pitch is not waterlogged, frozen or too hard.

REMEMBER

In addition to the above precautions, correct techniques must be used and coaches' instructions followed. Always be responsible for your own safety.

daydream
EDUCATION

INJURIES

Lots of different types of injuries can occur as a result of taking part in physical activities. Accidents and injuries will happen, so it is vital to be able to identify and treat various injuries. If you are ever in doubt, contact the emergency services.

CAUSES

Internally caused injuries
Caused by the individual performing the activity.

Overuse injuries occur when people train too hard or too often, causing continuous stress on the body. Examples include stress fractures, shin splints and tennis elbow.

Sudden injuries happen when people put strain on their body through overstretching, twisting or turning. Examples include pulled muscles and bone fractures.

Externally caused injuries
Caused by factors outside of the individual's control, such as the environment. These include:

- Foul play or incorrect actions by opponents
- Impact with equipment, the playing surface or opponents
- Inappropriate clothing and damaged or faulty equipment
- Very hot or cold weather conditions

COMMON INJURIES

Fractures – Broken or cracked bones result when the force on the bone is stronger than the bone itself.

Simple/Closed	Compound/Open	Stress	Greenstick
The bone does not break through the skin.	The broken bone breaks through the skin, creating a risk of infection.	A small crack occurs in a bone caused by an overuse injury.	The bone bends and breaks on the outside of the bone.

Joint Injuries – These injuries are found where two bones meet.

Dislocations	Tennis Elbow	Sprain	Torn Cartilage
One of the bones at a joint comes out of place, usually due to a fall or hard blow.	Tendons are inflamed due to overuse, causing pain on the outside of the elbow.	Fibres of a ligament are torn through overstretching, twisting or turning.	Tears appear in the cartilage at a joint. This commonly occurs at the knee.

Other Injuries – There are various other injuries that can result from physical activity.

Concussion	Open Soft Tissue	Closed Soft Tissue	Strain
An impact to the head causes unconsciousness, confusion or memory loss.	The skin is broken (e.g. through cuts or abrasions), causing blood to leave the body.	The skin is not broken so there is no external bleeding (e.g. strains and bruises).	A muscle or tendon is overstretched or torn.

The **RICE** principle is used to treat joint and soft tissue injuries to reduce swelling and pain.

R I C E
REST   ICE   COMPRESSION   ELEVATION

Rest – Stop taking part in physical activity and rest the injury.

Ice – Apply an ice pack to the injury.

Compression – Apply pressure and give support to the injury with a bandage. If the pressure is too tight, it may restrict blood flow.

Elevation – Raise the injured body part and keep it supported to reduce blood flow to the area and drain fluids.

daydream EDUCATION

PERFORMANCE-ENHANCING DRUGS

Performance-enhancing drugs can produce physical or psychological effects that improve performance. However, misuse of these drugs can pose significant health risks, and taking them is regarded as cheating.

BETA BLOCKERS

- Block the effects of adrenaline, lowering heart rate and anxiety.
- Reduce muscle tremors and shaking; increase focus.
- Advantageous in precision sports such as snooker, archery and shooting.

Possible side effects: dangerously low heart rate, low blood pressure, dizziness, nausea, diarrhoea, insomnia, sleep disturbances and tiredness.

NARCOTICS/ANALGESICS

- Temporarily reduce pain by depressing the central nervous system.
- Allow athletes to continue to compete whilst injured.
- Provide a sense of elation and being unbeatable.

Possible side effects: nausea, vomiting, constipation, low blood pressure, further damage to injury, addiction, and loss of concentration and coordination.

STIMULANTS

- Increase brain activity and enhance mental and physical alertness.
- Reduce fatigue and speed up reaction times.
- Advantageous in sports in which aggression is beneficial, such as boxing and rugby, and endurance events in which it can be difficult to stay focused for a long time, such as long-distance cycling.

Possible side effects: insomnia, irritability, anxiety, irregular heart rate, dehydration, high blood pressure and addiction.

DIURETICS

- Increase the rate of urine production and reduce the amount of fluid in the body, which helps performers lose weight.
- Reduce the concentration or mask the presence of other banned substances in urine.
- Advantageous in sports that have weight limits, such as boxing and horse racing.

Possible side effects: dehydration, dizziness, muscle pains or cramps, headaches, nausea, exhaustion, heart failure and kidney damage.

ANABOLIC STEROIDS

- Mimic the effects of the male sex hormone testosterone, which promotes muscle growth.
- Allow performers to train harder for longer, which improves strength.
- Speed up recovery time.
- Advantageous in sports that require strength and power such as sprinting and weightlifting.

Possible side effects: aggression and mood swings, acne, high blood pressure, liver damage, heart and circulatory problems, infertility and death.

PEPTIDE HORMONES

- Naturally occurring hormones that facilitate muscle growth and the production of red blood cells.

Erythropoietin (EPO)
- Increases production of red blood cells and the delivery of oxygen to working muscles.
- Advantageous in sports that require endurance such as long- distance running or cycling.

Possible side effects: thickened blood, stroke, heart attack, blood clots and seizures.

Human Growth Hormone (HGH)
- Increases muscle mass and improves strength.
- Advantageous in sports that require strength and power such as sprinting.

Possible side effects: arthritis, heart failure, high cholesterol, high blood pressure and diabetes.

Blood doping involves increasing the number of red blood cells in the blood stream to boost its oxygen-carrying capacity and improve performance. This can be done through drugs, such as EPO, or blood transfusions. *Possible side effects: kidney failure, thickened blood and heart attack.*

daydream EDUCATION

Health, Fitness & Well-Being

PHYSICAL HEALTH

Health Benefits

Regular physical activity can improve physical health and reduce health risks. As well as making everyday tasks easier, physical activity can provide other health benefits.

Health benefits include:

- Improved function of body organs
- Stronger muscles, bones and joints
- Reduced risk of obesity and associated health problems, such as osteoporosis, heart disease and diabetes
- Decreased blood pressure and cholesterol
- Increased life expectancy

Fitness Benefits

Regular physical activity can also improve fitness levels and physical ability.

Fitness benefits include:

- Greater strength and muscular endurance
- Improved cardiovascular fitness
- Greater flexibility
- Better performance

EMOTIONAL HEALTH

Emotional Benefits

Regular physical activity can help improve emotional health.

Emotional benefits include:

- Improved confidence and self-esteem
- Reduced risk of depression
- Relief from stress and tension
- Improved ability to deal with pressure and manage emotions
- Increased serotonin and endorphin levels, which help improve mood

SOCIAL HEALTH

Social Benefits

Regular physical activity can help improve social health.

Social benefits include:

- Opportunities to meet new friends and form new relationships
- Opportunities to catch up with existing friends
- Better leadership and teamwork skills
- Improved social skills

LIFESTYLE CHOICES

There are various lifestyle choices that can affect your health, including diet, activity level, work/rest/sleep balance and recreational drugs.

DIET

A balanced diet is key to maintaining a healthy lifestyle. A balanced diet involves eating the right balance of nutrients, and not just the right amount of food.

Eating too little can lead to **malnutrition.**

Possible Effects:

Muscle atrophy
Fatigue
Depression
Dizziness

Eating too much sugar, fat and salt can lead to **obesity.**

Possible Effects:

Diabetes
Heart disease
Osteoporosis
Mobility issues

SMOKING

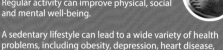

Possible effects on health:

- High blood pressure and heart rate
- Increased risk of coronary heart disease (CHD), lung cancer, bronchitis and emphysema
- Higher risk of complications during medical operations
- Can harm the health of those exposed to passive smoking

Possible effects on sporting performance:

- Tiredness and shortness of breath resulting from increased carbon monoxide in the blood and reduced oxygen-carrying capacity; makes it difficult to participate in endurance sports

ALCOHOL

Possible effects on health:

- Liver damage
- Weight gain and high blood pressure
- Psychological problems such as depression
- Higher risk of dehydration from extra urine production

Possible effects on sporting performance:

- Loss of concentration and coordination
- Mobility affected by excess weight
- Has calming effects and is banned in sports in which it could be beneficial
- Slows reaction times, impairs judgement and is banned in sports because of safety risk

ACTIVITY LEVEL

Regular activity can improve physical, social and mental well-being.

A sedentary lifestyle can lead to a wide variety of health problems, including obesity, depression, heart disease, diabetes, high blood pressure and an increased risk of osteoporosis.

Conversely, overtraining can negatively affect health so it is important to create personalised exercise programmes that include rest periods for recovery.

WORK/REST/SLEEP BALANCE

It is important to maintain a good work/rest/ sleep balance. Working too hard and a lack of sleep can cause:

- Stress and anxiety
- Depression
- Poor concentration
- High blood pressure
- Heart disease and strokes

Sleep helps with mental and physical recovery and is vital to a healthy lifestyle.

 daydream EDUCATION

WEIGHT-RELATED CONDITIONS

If you do not live a healthy active lifestyle and maintain a balanced diet, then you may suffer from a weight-related condition.

OPTIMUM WEIGHT

Optimum weight varies from person to person. The following factors affect a person's optimum weight:

| Height | Sex | Muscle Size | Bone Structure |

Think about how these can affect participation and performance levels.

Anorexia

Anorexia is a serious eating disorder. Sufferers refuse to eat due to a fixation on losing weight or a fear of gaining weight. This leads to sufferers becoming dangerously thin and having a serious lack of nutrition. Other health problems include:

- Fatigue
- Feeling lightheaded or dizzy
- Dehydration
- Depression or anxiety
- Muscle atrophy (muscles waste away)
- Death

Underweight

An underweight person weighs less than the healthy, expected weight for his or her height and sex. Being underweight can lead to health problems.

Some sports performers, such as jockeys, are deliberately underweight in an attempt to improve their performance. Weight loss can be achieved through exercising, wearing sweat suits, or taking drugs known as diuretics, which increase urine production and reduce the amount of liquid in the body. All of these methods can cause dehydration, which negatively affects health and performance.

Being anorexic or underweight can cause tiredness and weakness, which can affect a person's ability to take part in regular exercise. In turn, this results in reduced fitness and performance levels.

Overweight

A person who is overweight weighs more than is expected for his or her height and sex. However, being overweight is not harmful unless the person also has a high body fat content. It can be caused by overeating, lack of activity or medical reasons.

Someone could also be overweight because they have a large muscle mass or bone structure. This can be beneficial in some sports such as rugby, in which extra muscle mass can help improve performance.

Overfat

Overfat describes someone who has a high body fat content and might be overweight. Being overfat can lead to health problems such as high blood pressure and high cholesterol levels.

It is possible for someone to be overweight without being overfat. For example, a weightlifter may be overweight, but not overfat, because of high levels of muscle mass. Similarly, it is also possible to be overfat but not overweight.

Obesity

An obese person is overweight and has extremely high body fat levels. Obesity can result from eating too much, a lack of physical activity and genetic factors. It can lead to serious health problems, including:

- Psychological problems such as depression
- Extra stress on bones and joints
- Type 2 diabetes
- Mobility issues
- Strokes
- Some types of cancer
- Osteoarthritis
- Heart disease

Being overweight, overfat or obese can cause discomfort, mobility issues and medical problems that limit a person's ability to take part in regular exercise.

NUTRITION

The energy and nutrients needed by your body to grow and stay healthy come from the air you breathe, the food you eat and the fluids you drink.

NUTRIENTS

Carbohydrates – the body's main source of energy

Simple carbs digest quickly and cause spikes in blood sugar and energy levels.

Complex carbs digest slowly and keep blood sugar levels stable.

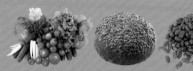

Fats – another source of energy for the body

Saturated and trans fats increase cholesterol and the risk of heart disease, diabetes and other health problems.

Not all fats are bad for you. Good fats can help lower cholesterol, reduce blood pressure and improve overall health.

Proteins – essential nutrients that the body uses for growth and repair

Proteins are broken down into amino acids during digestion, and the body uses them to build new cells, repair tissue and produce antibodies.

Water

Water is essential for the body. It is involved in every bodily function and makes up over half of your body weight! A lack of water can lead to dehydration and other health problems.

Fibre

Fibre is not a nutrient, but it is an important part of a healthy diet and is essential for digestive health. It can help prevent heart disease, diabetes, weight gain and some cancers.

46

daydream
EDUCATION

Vitamins and Minerals – essential for a healthy body and to prevent certain diseases

Fruit and vegetables are packed full of vitamins and minerals.

B Vitamins

Help with the release of energy and the repair of tissue.

Vitamin C

Helps protect the body from infection, heal wounds and absorb minerals from food.

Calcium

Important for the growth of strong bones and teeth in children.

Iron

Needed for the formation of red blood cells.

A BALANCED DIET

A balanced diet that contains a variety of different foods and nutrients is essential for maintaining a healthy lifestyle.

A guideline for a healthy diet is shown below.

Fruit and vegetables

A great source of fibre and a variety of vitamins and minerals; generally low in fat.

Potatoes, bread, rice, pasta and other starchy carbohydrates

High in carbohydrates, but wholegrain varieties are a great source of fibre and protein.

Oils and spreads

Choose unsaturated oils and use in small amounts.

Fatty and sugary foods

High in fat and sugar. Eat less often and in small amounts.

Beans, pulses, fish, eggs, meat and other proteins

A great source of protein, iron and zinc; choose lean cuts of meat to reduce fat intake.

Dairy and alternatives

A great source of calcium and protein but can be high in fat.

SPECIFIC SPORTS NUTRITION

A balanced diet is one that includes a variety of foods and nutrients. However, sometimes, a diet may need to be adapted to maximise athletic performance.

LEVEL OF PARTICIPATION

Eating food provides the body with energy. Therefore, the amount of food and energy you need depends on your level of participation in physical activity – the more exercise you do, the more food you will need.

– Negative

If you eat less food than you need, your body will use up its fat reserves and you will lose weight.

Energy Balance

+ Positive

If you eat more food than you need, the surplus will be stored as fat and you will gain weight.

If you go above or under your optimum body weight, it can affect your performance in sport.

WHEN TO EAT

It is vital to consume the right foods at the right time when exercising.

When you exercise, your working muscles need more oxygen and nutrients. As a result, blood is diverted from inactive areas, such as your stomach, to the working muscles. This is called **blood shunting.**

The blood vessels leading to the working muscles get bigger (**vasodilation**), and the blood vessels leading to inactive areas constrict (**vasoconstriction**). This is why it is important not to eat too close to exercising.

Before Exercise
Try to wait two hours after eating a meal before exercising. If you exercise too soon after eating, you may have insufficient energy or develop stomach pains.

During Exercise
Generally you should not eat during exercise. However, a small snack is sometimes needed during endurance activities.

After Exercise
Eat complex carbohydrates to replace the energy used during exercise. Protein will help rebuild and maintain muscle tissue.

Drink water before, during and after exercise to replace lost liquids and avoid dehydration.

DIFFERENT DIETS FOR DIFFERENT SPORTS

High-protein Diets

Proteins are broken down into amino acids, which help grow and repair muscle tissue. High-protein foods can be difficult to digest and should be avoided before training or competing.

Meat, fish, eggs, milk, beans, whole grains and nuts are all generally high in protein.

Sports performers that need power and strength, such as weightlifters, rugby players and sprinters, adopt high-protein diets to build muscle and lose fat.

Carbo-loading

Carbo-loading increases the amount of glycogen stored in the muscles and provides a slow-release form of energy that helps to delay tiredness.

Carbohydrates can be found in foods such as pasta, bread, rice and potatoes.

Endurance athletes, such as marathon runners, increase their carbohydrate intake in the lead-up to a race or competition to improve performance during the end of a race.

daydream EDUCATION

CLASSIFICATION OF SKILLS

Skills can be classified on continuums. This enables them to be practised in the most effective way.

THE ENVIRONMENTAL CONTINUUM

 **Skills can be:** **OPEN** OR **CLOSED**

- Affected by the environment
- Involve decision making
- Externally paced

- Not affected by the environment
- The skill is habitual
- Self paced

THE DIFFICULTY CONTINUUM

 **Skills can be:** **BASIC** OR **COMPLEX**

- Little information to process
- Few decisions to make
- Used in many sports

- Lots of information to process
- Decisions need to be made quickly
- Generally sport specific

THE ORGANISATION CONTINUUM

 **Skills can be:** **LOW** OR **HIGH**

- Uncomplicated and simple
- Involve subroutines that are usually discrete
- Subroutines can be practised separately and then integrated into the whole skill

- Complex and require large amounts of attention
- Involve closely integrated subroutines that are difficult to separate
- Best practiced as a whole

PRACTICE METHODS

Massed	*Variable*	*Fixed*	*Distributed*
Good for basic skills	**Good for open skills**	**Good for closed skills**	**Good for new or complex skills**
The skill is repeated continuously with little or no rest until the skill is developed.	The environment changes. Decisions have to be made quickly.	The skill is repeated in a stable environment. It becomes habitual.	The skill is practised in a number of short sessions.

49

SMART Targets

When you train, it is important to set targets and goals.
Setting **SMART** targets will help you:
- *Stay motivated and focused*
- *Monitor your progress*
- *Plan your training sessions*

S — SPECIFIC

Clearly explain what you want to achieve and ensure your target is specific and relevant.

✓ **Specific** – *I want to improve my pass completion percentage.*

✗ **Vague** – *I want to be better at hockey.*

M — MEASURABLE

Set measurable targets so you can track your progress and measure if your target has been achieved.

✓ **Measurable** – *I want to improve my 50-km time by five minutes.*

✗ **Unmeasurable** – *I want to be better at cycling.*

A — ACHIEVABLE

Set targets that you have the ability to reach. Unattainable targets are demotivating and result in failure.

✓ **Achievable** – *I want to improve my shooting accuracy by 10%.*

✗ **Unachievable** – *I want my shooting accuracy to be 100%.*

R — REALISTIC

Ensure your target is realistic for you personally. Factors, such as work and hobbies, affect your ability to meet your targets. As such, the second target below is likely to be unrealistic.

✓ **Realistic** – *I want to train three days a week.*

✗ **Unrealistic** – *I want to train seven days a week.*

T — TIMED

Create a timeframe for you to achieve your targets. Set an end point as a deadline for achieving your final goal. Establishing a timescale can also help you stay focused.

✓ **Timed** – *I want to beat my personal best (PB) within two months.*

✗ **Not timed** – *I want to improve my swimming.*

Having SMART targets will motivate you to stay on track!

*Always check that your targets are **SMART!***

☑ Specific ☑ Measurable ☑ Achievable ☑ Realistic ☑ Timed

50

 daydream EDUCATION

GUIDANCE

There are four main types of guidance that are used to assist in the learning process.

VISUAL GUIDANCE

Practical demonstrations, diagrams and other visual prompts are used to help the learner create a mental image of the skill that needs to be learned.

+ Helps the learner visualise the skill
+ Can be used at all stages of learning but most effective at the early stages
+ Skills can be broken down into parts (sub-routines) to highlight the technical stages

- Must be accurate and technically correct
- Complex skills can be very difficult for a learner to comprehend
- Static visual aids may not provide enough guidance or information

VERBAL GUIDANCE

A spoken explanation of how a skill is performed is provided. It is often used with advanced learners who are in the final stages of learning the skill.

+ Effective when used in conjunction with other forms of guidance
+ Good for advanced performers
+ Can be provided during a performance and is ideal for open skills

- Explanations must be clear and concise not to confuse the learner
- Must limit the amount of information
- Complex and high organisational skills are very difficult to explain verbally

MANUAL GUIDANCE

The teacher or coach physically moves the body of the learner through the correct pattern of movement. For example, a coach may guide a performer through a forehand tennis shot.

+ Can be used with learners of all abilities
+ Helps the learner gain a kinaesthetic sense of the movement
+ Helps build confidence

- The learner can become dependent on the guidance
- Difficult when working with large groups

MECHANICAL GUIDANCE

Equipment is used to help the learner practise a skill – for example, a new swimmer using a float.

+ Very effective in the early stages of leaning
+ Helps the learner gain a kinaesthetic sense of the movement
+ Helps build confidence

- The learner can become dependent on the guidance
- The movement experienced with guidance may be different to the actual movement

FEEDBACK

Feedback is information received about a performance. It can be positive or negative, and can have a big impact on performance.

TYPES OF FEEDBACK

Intrinsic

Intrinsic feedback is based on how a performance felt to the performer.

Experienced performers will know when something feels right or wrong, whereas beginners may not have such experience.

Extrinsic

Extrinsic feedback comes from another person who saw the performance, such as a coach.

Beginners will benefit greatly from extrinsic feedback as they may not have the knowledge to assess their own performance.

Concurrent feedback is provided **during** the performance.
Terminal feedback is provided **before or after** the performance.

Feedback can focus on the technical performance or the results of a performance.

Knowledge of Performance (KP)

Examining the execution of the movements performed (technique) enables performers to assess the correctness of their movements. For example, a golfer watching a video of his or her last practice swing.

Knowledge of Result (KR)

Examining performance results enables performers to analyse their performance and compare it to previous performances. For example, race times in track events, pass completion rates in netball or tackles made in rugby.

INFORMATION PROCESSING MODEL

Feedback is part of the Information Processing Model.

INPUT Senses → **DECISION MAKING** Brain → **OUTPUT** Body

FEEDBACK

Example: Football free kick
Input: *Goalkeeper positioned left, wall too far right, no wind.*
Decision Making: *Use experience and skill to determine where to kick the ball.*
Output: *Kick ball hard with dip into the top right corner of the goal.*
Feedback: *KR – no goal, too high; KP – felt good, more dip next time.*

daydream EDUCATION

MENTAL PREPARATION

In order to perform at the optimum level, you need to ensure that you are mentally prepared.

AROUSAL

Arousal refers to your level of excitement and readiness to perform.

If your arousal level is too low, you are not likely to be driven or motivated enough to perform at your optimum level.

If your arousal level is too high, you are likely to get nervous, anxious or over-aggressive.

Optimum arousal level varies for different sports.

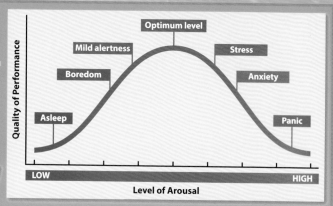

Quality of Performance — Level of Arousal (LOW to HIGH)

Asleep · Boredom · Mild alertness · Optimum level · Stress · Anxiety · Panic

The optimum arousal level for sports that require fine motor skills, such as snooker, is relatively low. Conversely, the optimum arousal level for sports that require gross motor skills and aggression, such as rugby, is relatively high. Therefore, it is important to mentally prepare specifically for your chosen activity.

MENTAL PREPARATION

Various mental preparation techniques can be used to help you reach optimum arousal level before a sporting activity.

1. Maintain a Positive Attitude

Use self-talk and positive imagery to create a positive frame of mind.

2. Mental Rehearsal

Visualise performing the activity or skill successfully to boost confidence.

3. Stay Calm

Listen to music and practise deep breathing to relax and reduce anxiety.

4. Eliminate Distractions

Ignore external factors that may cause stress or anxiety.

MOTIVATION

Motivation also greatly affects performance. It can either be intrinsic or extrinsic:

Intrinsic

Internally driven motivation that is linked to enjoyment, pride and satisfaction.

Extrinsic

Externally driven motivation that is linked to praise or rewards such as trophies or money.

Both are effective motivators for success. However, unless you have the internal drive and desire to succeed, it can be difficult to remain motivated.

Always remember to perform a full warm-up to prepare for physical activity!

daydream EDUCATION

53

INFLUENCES ON PARTICIPATION

There are various factors that influence participation in physical activity.

PEOPLE

Family
Parents, siblings and other relatives may encourage you to take part in particular activities and offer financial and emotional support.

Peers
Friends, classmates and members of your sports club may encourage you to play the sports that interest them and avoid others.

Role Models
Famous sportspeople or good performers at your school or sports club may inspire you to compete in specific sports.

GENDER

Women's participation levels in sport are increasing. However, there are still fewer women participating in sport than men, particularly in football and golf. Biased media coverage, fewer opportunities and stereotyping are all blamed for this.

Men's sport dominates the media, with women's events receiving a much lower profile. This contributes to fewer opportunities and less funding for women and fewer female role models.

Some sports are also associated with either men or women (gender tagging). For example, some consider netball to be a feminine sport, and boxing to be a masculine sport. These perceptions can influence a person's decision to participate in a given sport.

ETHNICITY AND RELIGION

Ethnicity and religious beliefs can have a big impact on participation in sport.

Some religions have strict guidelines that may affect religious people's decision to participate in sport. For example, some Christians will not participate in sport on a Sunday.

Unfortunately, racism is still an issue in sport despite huge efforts to promote racial equality.

SOCIO-ECONOMIC GROUP

People are less likely to participate in sport if they are from a low socio-economic group. Some sports are inexpensive and easily accessible. However, others, such as golf and skiing, require expensive clothing, equipment and club membership, which can prevent people from taking part.

Particular sports, such as golf, have a certain status that makes people want to play them.

AGE

Age can affect a person's ability to participate in certain activities.

For example, weight lifting can be damaging to children, whereas physical sports, such as rugby, can be too demanding for elderly people. As a result, people of different ages will participate in different sports.

DISABILITY

A disability may affect a person's ability to participate in certain activities. However, many sports, such as basketball (wheelchair basketball), have been adapted to enable people with disabilities to participate.

Events such as the Paralympics have helped raise the profile of disabled sports.

daydream
EDUCATION

COMMERCIALISATION

The commercialisation of sport involves the sale, display or use of sport to generate income.

Sport is a multibillion-pound industry, with sporting events and performers attracting huge media interest and sponsorship deals. Sports, the media and sponsors all benefit from, and are dependent on, one another.

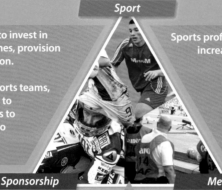

Sport

Sports use the money to invest in facilities, players, coaches, provision and their own promotion.

Companies sponsor sports teams, events and performers to promote their products to a wider audience and to enhance their image.

Sports profit financially and benefit from increased awareness and exposure.

The media pays for the rights to broadcast sporting events.

Media coverage can inspire people to participate in sport.

Sponsorship

Media

The media provides sponsors with a wider audience to promote their product or service to. This can result in greater sponsorship for sports.

Negative Effects of the Commercialisation of Sport

Sports

- The most popular sports and top-tier teams and players benefit the most.
- Lesser sports, teams and players struggle to compete.
- The media can influence the scheduling and format of sports to make them more audience friendly.

Sponsors

- Poor performance or behaviour can lead to negative press.
- Small companies struggle to compete with large companies.
- Some sponsors' products may not be appropriate for the sport or the general audience (e.g. cigarettes).

Media

- The broadcasting rights for large sporting events are very expensive.
- Small media companies cannot compete with larger companies.

Spectators

- Attending sporting events can be expensive.
- Encourages spectating as opposed to participation.
- More adverts and possible disruption to fixtures list.

Performers

- Contractual obligations, such as attending events or appearing in adverts.
- Performers are sometimes contractually prohibited from using competitors' products.
- Performers may become motivated primarily by money and a desire for fame.

Sporting Behaviour

SPORTSMANSHIP

As well as having rules, sports often have codes of conduct and etiquette to ensure that players are honest and respectful to their opponents. This is known as sportsmanship.

Sportsmanship involves ethical, appropriate, polite and fair behaviour while participating in sporting activities.

Examples:
A cricketer 'walking' before officially being given out.
A footballer kicking the ball out of play when another player is injured.
Tennis players shaking hands at the end of a game.

GAMESMANSHIP

Gamesmanship involves the use of 'unfair' tactics to gain an advantage in a sporting activity. It involves pushing the rules to the limit without breaking them. Therefore, it usually goes unpunished.

Examples:
Deliberately losing a game to get an 'easier' draw in a competition.
Wasting time to break up the flow of a game or run down the clock.
Faking an injury in any sporting activity.

DEVIANCE

Sporting deviance is behaviour that falls outside the laws of a sport or is deemed unacceptable. All sports have rules to discourage deviance, but due to the high-pressure nature of sport, it is still rife.

Examples of deviance include:

| Performance-enhancing drugs | Violent conduct | Match fixing | Professional fouls |

Reasons for deviance:

| High pressure to win | Lack of moral constraint | Rewards of winning are too high | "Win at all cost" mentality |

Depending on the severity of deviance, punishments vary. For example, a minor infringement such as a professional foul is often punished with a warning. Alternatively, taking drugs or fixing matches can result in a permanent ban or even a prison sentence.

Why do you think deviance is more common in elite-level sport?

daydream EDUCATION

Notes